Specific Skill Series

Following Directions

Richard A. Boning

Fifth Edition

SRA/McGraw-Hill

Columbus, Ohio

Cover, Back Cover, ZEFA/Germany/The Stock Market

SRA/McGraw-Hill

A Division of The **McGraw·Hill** *Companies*

Printed in the United States of America.

Send all inquiries to:
    SRA/McGraw-Hill
    8787 Orion Place
    Columbus, OH 43240-4027

ISBN 0-02-687929-8

    5 6 7 IPC 03 02 01

To the Teacher

PURPOSE:

FOLLOWING DIRECTIONS is designed to develop skill in reading, understanding, and following instructions and directions. Proficiency in this basic skill is essential for success in every school subject and in nonacademic activities as well.

FOR WHOM:

The skill of FOLLOWING DIRECTIONS is developed through a series of books spanning ten levels (Picture, Preparatory, A, B, C, D, E, F, G, H). The Picture Level is for pupils who have not acquired a basic sight vocabulary. The Preparatory Level is for pupils who have a basic sight vocabulary but are not yet ready for the first-grade-level book. Books A through H are appropriate for pupils who can read on levels one through eight, respectively. **The use of the *Specific Skill Series Placement Test* is recommended to determine the appropriate level.**

THE NEW EDITION:

The fifth edition of the *Specific Skill Series* maintains the quality and focus that has distinguished this program for more than 25 years. A key element central to the program's success has been the unique nature of the reading selections. Nonfiction pieces about current topics have been designed to stimulate the interest of students, motivating them to use the comprehension strategies they have learned to further their reading. To keep this important aspect of the program intact, a percentage of the reading selections have been replaced in order to ensure the continued relevance of the subject material.

In addition, a significant percentage of the artwork in the program has been replaced to give the books a contemporary look. The cover photographs are designed to appeal to readers of all ages.

SESSIONS:

Short practice sessions are the most effective. It is desirable to have a practice session every day or every other day, using a few units each session.

SCORING:

Pupils should record their answers on the reproducible worksheets. The worksheets make scoring easier and provide uniform records of the pupils' work. Using worksheets also avoids consuming the exercise books.

It is important for pupils to know how well they are doing. For this reason, units should be scored as soon as they have been completed. Then a discussion can be held in which pupils justify their choices. (The Integrated Language Activities, many of which are open-ended, do not lend themselves to an objective score; thus there are no answer keys for these pages.)

GENERAL INFORMATION ON *FOLLOWING DIRECTIONS*:

FOLLOWING DIRECTIONS focuses attention on four types of directions. The *testing and drilling* directions are like those in most textbooks and workbooks. Mastery of this type, so vital to school success, is stressed throughout FOLLOWING DIRECTIONS. The second type of direction is found in science books and involves *experimenting*. Such material requires the reader to find an answer to a problem or provides the reader with an example of practical application of a principle.

The third type of direction, *assembling*, deals with parts or ingredients and the order and way in which they are put together. Here the purpose is to make or create, rather than to solve a problem or demonstrate a principle.

Directions which tell how to do something are *performing* directions. They accent the steps in learning to do something new. The focus is on the performance rather than on the product.

SUGGESTED STEPS:

On levels A-H, pupils read the information above the first line. Then they answer the questions *below* this line. (Pupils are *not* to respond in writing to information *above* the first line; they are only to study it. Pupils should not write or mark anything in this book.) On the Picture Level, pupils tell if a picture correctly follows the directions. On the Preparatory Level, pupils tell which picture out of two correctly follows the directions.

Additional information on using FOLLOWING DIRECTIONS with pupils will be found in the **Specific Skill Series Teacher's Manual**.

RELATED MATERIALS:

Specific Skill Series Placement Tests, which enable the teacher to place pupils at their appropriate levels in each skill, are available for the Elementary (Pre-1–6) and Midway (4–8) grade levels.

Following directions is an important part of your life. At home, your parents may say, "Put away your toys." In school, your teacher may say, "Write your name at the top of your paper." On the street, the crossing guard may say, "Do not cross yet."

Following directions is like trying to find your way with a map. If you follow the map correctly, you will get where you want to go. If you make a mistake, you will get lost.

It is important to understand directions. It is important to follow them correctly.

Think about directions carefully. Ask yourself questions like these: What do the directions tell me to do? Do I understand all the words in the directions? Should I do one thing before I do another?

In this book, you will read directions to do something. Under each direction is a picture. Ask yourself, "Is the person in the picture following the directions?" Then answer the question, "Is this right?" Choose **Yes** if the person is following the directions. Choose **No** if the person is not following the directions.

DIRECTIONS:

Play ball.

Is this right?

(A) Yes   **(B) No**

DIRECTIONS:

Cut the wood.

Is this right?

(A) Yes   **(B) No**

DIRECTIONS:

Look at TV.

Is this right?

(A) Yes   **(B) No**

DIRECTIONS:

Stay in the boat.

Is this right?

(A) Yes   **(B) No**

DIRECTIONS:

Walk the dog.

Is this right?

(A) Yes   **(B) No**

DIRECTIONS:

Sit on the bed.

Is this right?

(A) Yes   **(B) No**

DIRECTIONS:

Put on your coat.

Is this right?

(A) Yes   **(B) No**

DIRECTIONS:

Help the cat.

Is this right?

(A) Yes   **(B) No**

DIRECTIONS:

Do not run.

Is this right?

(A) Yes   **(B) No**

DIRECTIONS:

Stop playing.

Is this right?

(A) Yes **(B) No**

DIRECTIONS:

Paint the bike.

Is this right?

(A) Yes   **(B) No**

DIRECTIONS:

Put the ball down.

Is this right?

(A) Yes   **(B) No**

A. Exercising Your Skill

Follow these directions. Write on your own paper.

UP	Draw an arrow that points **up**.
DOWN	Draw an arrow that points **down**.
LEFT	Draw an arrow that points **left**.
RIGHT	Draw an arrow that points **right**.

B. Expanding Your Skill

Draw five circles in a row.
Make the sides of the circles touch.
Put a face on a circle at one end.
Color your caterpillar.

C. Exploring Language

In a row, draw one box for each letter in your name.

Write your name with one letter in each box.

Draw little circles under the boxes.

Color your name train.

D. Expressing Yourself

What could this be? Draw the same shape on your paper. Make it into something. Tell a story about it.

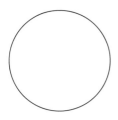

What could this be? Draw the same shape on your paper. Make it into something. Tell a story about it.

DIRECTIONS:

Jump into the water.

Is this right?

(A) Yes   **(B) No**

DIRECTIONS:

Do not pet the goat.

Is this right?

(A) Yes   **(B) No**

DIRECTIONS:

Walk with Mother.

Is this right?

(A) Yes   **(B) No**

DIRECTIONS:

Get into the car.

Is this right?

(A) Yes   **(B) No**

DIRECTIONS:

Look at the train.

Is this right?

(A) Yes **(B) No**

DIRECTIONS:

Make a boat.

Is this right?

(A) Yes   **(B) No**

DIRECTIONS:

Take something to read.

Is this right?

(A) Yes   **(B) No**

DIRECTIONS:

Ride with Mother.

Is this right?

(A) Yes   **(B) No**

DIRECTIONS:

Do the work.

Is this right?

(A) Yes **(B) No**

DIRECTIONS:

Help me ride.

Is this right?

(A) Yes   **(B) No**

DIRECTIONS:

Love your dog.

Is this right?

(A) Yes   **(B) No**

DIRECTIONS:

Sail the boat.

Is this right?

(A) Yes   **(B) No**

A. Exercising Your Skill

Look at the picture.

Tell what the boy is doing.

1. Count the number of letters in the word **puzzle**. Write the number with a red crayon.

2. Count how many times you see the letter **z** in the word **puzzle**. Write the number with a blue crayon.

B. Expanding Your Skill

Make a puzzle.

1. Write your name on a sheet of paper. Use a crayon. Make your name big.

2. Cut the paper into five parts. Give the parts to a friend. See if the friend can put the puzzle together again.

C. Exploring Language

Look at this puzzle. Can you tell which letters are missing?

a	b		d	e			h

Use a pencil to copy the letters above on your own paper. Leave a space for each missing letter. Then add the missing letters in the places where they go. Write them with a red crayon.

D. Expressing Yourself

Do one of these things.

1. Make a hidden letter picture. First, write one letter on a sheet of paper. Then make the letter into a picture that hides the letter. See if a friend can find the letter in your drawing.

2. Write a part of the alphabet. Leave two letters out. See if a friend can figure out which letters are missing.

DIRECTIONS:

Stay in bed.

Is this right?

(A) Yes   **(B) No**

DIRECTIONS:

Do not walk in the rain.

Is this right?

(A) Yes   **(B) No**

DIRECTIONS:

Sit in the boat.

Is this right?

(A) Yes   **(B) No**

DIRECTIONS:

Run home.

Is this right?

(A) Yes   **(B) No**

DIRECTIONS:

Sit up.

Is this right?

(A) Yes   **(B) No**

DIRECTIONS:

Talk to the man.

Is this right?

(A) Yes   **(B) No**

DIRECTIONS:

Stop the dog.

Is this right?

(A) Yes   **(B) No**

DIRECTIONS:

Help the girl.

Is this right?

(A) Yes   **(B) No**

DIRECTIONS:

Let the cat go.

Is this right?

(A) Yes   **(B) No**

DIRECTIONS:

Do not eat.

Is this right?

(A) Yes **(B) No**

DIRECTIONS:

Take some cake.

Is this right?

(A) Yes   **(B) No**

DIRECTIONS:

Show Mother the book.

Is this right?

(A) Yes (B) No

DIRECTIONS:

Ride in the road.

Is this right?

(A) Yes   **(B) No**

DIRECTIONS:

Get out of the tree.

Is this right?

(A) Yes **(B) No**

A. Exercising Your Skill

Find the secret message.
Copy the letters.
Circle the small letters.
Do not circle capital
letters.

tiBVRsfAEuRnOPLTtorEXCWeaWFCdD

Write a capital **I** on your paper. Then write the letters you circled. Leave spaces between some letters so they make a pattern like this:

I__ __ __ __ __ __ __ __ __ __ __ __ __.

Read the secret message.

B. Expanding Your Skill

Think of something you can do. Can you tell someone else how to do it? Give someone else some directions to follow. Tell what to do first, second, third, and so forth.

C. Exploring Language

Can you read this?　　I

　　　　　　　　　　　nac

　　　　　　　　　　　daer

　　　　　　　　　　　a

　　　　　　　　　　　.koob

The words in this message are backward. Write each word on your paper, putting the last letter first, the next-to-the-last letter second, and so forth. After you have written all the words, read the message or have someone read it to you.

D. Expressing Yourself

Think of a story you have heard. Draw a picture of something that happens in the story. Use five colors in your picture. Write the name of the story at the top of the page.

DIRECTIONS:

Work with Father.

Is this right?

(A) Yes　　　　**(B) No**

DIRECTIONS:

Paint the car.

Is this right?

(A) Yes   **(B) No**

DIRECTIONS:

Put the cat out.

Is this right?

(A) Yes   **(B) No**

DIRECTIONS:

Look at the little pig.

Is this right?

(A) Yes   **(B) No**

DIRECTIONS:

Go into the house.

Is this right?

(A) Yes **(B) No**

DIRECTIONS:

Make it look new.

Is this right?

(A) Yes (B) No

DIRECTIONS:

Play with the dog.

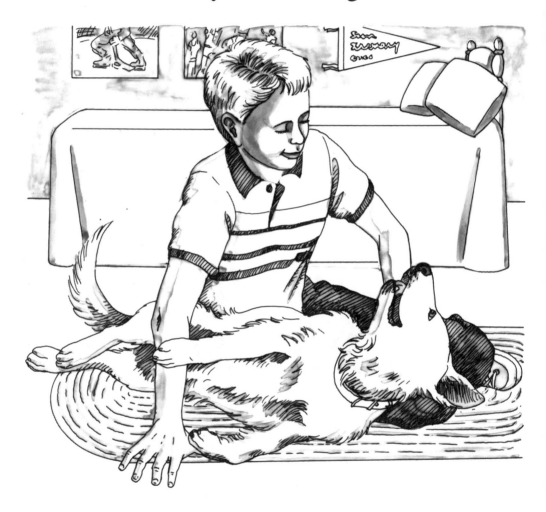

Is this right?

(A) Yes　　　　　**(B) No**

DIRECTIONS:

Do not read in bed.

Is this right?

(A) Yes   **(B) No**

DIRECTIONS:

Stay home.

Is this right?

(A) Yes **(B) No**

DIRECTIONS:

Help the baby.

Is this right?

(A) Yes   **(B) No**

DIRECTIONS:

Run with the ball.

Is this right?

(A) Yes   **(B) No**

DIRECTIONS:

Eat a hot dog.

Is this right?

(A) Yes   **(B) No**

A. Exercising Your Skill

Find the animal names.

First, copy the letters below.

Draw a circle around every other letter.

Start with the first letter in each group.

Write each animal name.

p l i t g   c r a s t   r e a v b i b e i r t

B. Expanding Your Skill

Draw a pig in a box.

Draw a cat in a circle.

Draw a rabbit in a triangle.

C. Exploring Language

See how many animal names you can find. Look across. Look up and down. On your paper, write each animal name you find.

n	d	o	g	c
l	u	y	x	o
e	c	a	t	w
p	k	i	o	u

D. Expressing Yourself

Draw mixed-up animals with a friend.

1. Fold a piece of paper in half. Have your friend do the same.

2. Draw the head of an animal above the fold, on the top half of your paper. Have your friend do the same.

3. Trade papers. Don't look at the top half yet.

4. Draw a body below the fold.

5. Open the page to see the head and body. Give the mixed-up animals funny names.